# THE SCIENCE OF **SUPERPOWERS**

# THE SCIENCE OF
# INVISIBILITY AND
# X-RAY VISION

Kaitlin Scirri

Cavendish Square

New York

D1568322

**Dedication**
To Marc, For your love of science and love of me. Thank you for all your support.

Published in 2019 by Cavendish Square Publishing, LLC
243 5th Avenue, Suite 136, New York, NY 10016

Copyright © 2019 by Cavendish Square Publishing, LLC

First Edition

Website: cavendishsq.com

This publication represents the opinions and views of the author based on his or her personal experience, knowledge, and research. The information in this book serves as a general guide only. The author and publisher have used their best efforts in preparing this book and disclaim liability rising directly or indirectly from the use and application of this book.

All websites were avai 3 1969 02669 9560 was sent to press.

Library of Congress Cataloging-in-Publication Data

Names: Scirri, Kaitlin, author.
Title: The science of invisibility and X-ray vision / Kaitlin Scirri.
Description: First edition. | New York : Cavendish Square, 2019. | Series: The science of superpowers | Includes bibliographical references and index. | Audience: Grades 3-6.
Identifiers: LCCN 2017048047 (print) | LCCN 2017049938 (ebook) | ISBN 9781502637901 (library bound) | ISBN 9781502637918 (pbk.) | ISBN 9781502637925 (ebook)
Subjects: LCSH: Invisibility--Juvenile literature. | Science--Miscellanea--Juvenile literature. | X-rays--Juvenile literature. | Vision--Juvenile literature. | Animals--Adaptations--Juvenile literature.
Classification: LCC QC406 (ebook) | LCC QC406 .S35 2019 (print) | DDC 502--dc23
LC record available at https://lccn.loc.gov/2017048047

Editorial Director: David McNamara
Editor: Kristen Susienka
Copy Editor: Rebecca Rohan
Associate Art Director: Amy Greenan
Designer: Joe Parenteau
Production Coordinator: Karol Szymczuk
Photo Research: J8 Media

The photographs in this book are used by permission and through the courtesy of: Cover Jennifer Hardt, Sweethardt Photography/Moment/Getty Images; p. 3 (and throughout the book) Keith Pomakis/Wikimedia Commons/File:Cumulus Clouds Over Jamaica.jpg/CC BY SA 2.5; p. 4 Serhii Bobyk/Shutterstock.com; p. 8 United Archives GmbH/Alamy Stock Photo; p. 9 Collection Christophel/Alamy Stock Photo; p. 11 Bettman/Getty Images; p. 12 Culture Club/Hulton Archive/Getty Images; p. 14 Goldmund/Getty Images; p. 19 Simonkr/E+/Getty Images; p. 20 Quisp65/Digital Vision/Getty Images; p. 21 Chinasong/Shutterstock.com; p. 22 Sgt. Jose Ramirez/Wikimedia Commons/file:Iron Knights at Night 150124-A-AG877-391.jpg/Public Domain; p. 24 TomekD76/iStock/Thinkstock; p. 27 Xantuanx/iStockphoto.com; p. 28 Gregory A. Pozhvanov/Shutterstock.com; p. 30 Dante Fenolio/Science Source/Getty Images; p. 32 Kuttelvaserova Stuchelova/Shutterstock.com; p. 33 Paul Reeves Photography/Shutterstock.com; p. 34 Eugen Haag/Shutterstock.com; p. 38 Yauhen_D/Shutterstock.com; p. 39 Cristina Arias/Cover/Getty Images; p. 40 United States Air Force/Wikimedia Commons/File:419th Flight Test Squadron - B-2 Spirit.jpg/Public Domain; p. 42 Nick Veasey/Untitled X-Ray/Getty Images.

Printed in the United States of America

# CONTENTS

# CHAPTER 1

# THE HISTORY OF INVISIBILITY AND X-RAY VISION

**E**ver since humans learned how to tell stories, there have been tales of people with incredible abilities. Some people can fly. Other people are super fast or super strong. And others can turn invisible or see through walls. People enjoy these stories.

*Opposite*: Magic helmets were common in ancient stories of invisibility.

However, could people ever do these things in real life? This is not an easy question to answer. There are people who are working to make these superpowers possible today. There are also some animals that seem to have some of these superpowers. If you could have a superpower, what would it be? Two of the most popular answers to that question are invisibility and X-ray vision.

## MYTHOLOGY AND STORYTELLING

Mythology is filled with stories of people and objects who had the powers of invisibility or X-ray vision. Magic helmets were common in Greek and Norse mythology. In Greek myths, the god Hades owned a helmet that could make whoever wore it invisible. That person could then sneak up on an enemy and win a battle. In Norse mythology, there was a helmet called the Tarnhelm. It could also make the wearer invisible. In Greek mythology, the god Lynceus could see through objects like trees and large rocks to find and defeat his enemies.

Stories about invisibility were included in Greek **philosophy** too. Philosophy is the study of knowledge and reasoning or a certain way of thinking. Around 370 BCE, the Greek philosopher

# CTs and MRIs

Since the discovery of the X-ray, other people have created new methods of looking inside an object or someone's body. A CT scan stands for a Computed Tomography scan. It works like an X-ray. A CT machine moves around a patient's body to get X-ray images from all sides. Another way of looking inside an object or someone's body is called an MRI. MRI stands for Magnetic Resonance Imaging. MRIs do not use X-rays and **radiation** to gather images like CT scans do. MRIs show more details and are better for viewing muscles and organs. CT scans and X-rays are better for viewing bones.

Plato wrote of a magical ring in his book *Republic*. The ring was called the Ring of Gyges. It could make the wearer invisible. The idea of a magical invisibility ring is also found in J.R.R. Tolkien's Lord of the Rings book series. The rings in these stories were meant to be a warning. Someone with rings like these would have a lot of power. Plato and Tolkien were trying to teach the lesson that too much power is dangerous and can lead to bad things.

The ring in the Lord of the Rings series makes the wearer invisible. This image from the movie shows character Frodo about to put on the ring.

Stories about superpowers have been popular for hundreds of years. Some of these stories were passed down from one family member to another. Others were written down in books or short stories. In 1897, a writer named H.G. Wells wrote a book called *The Invisible Man*. It was a story about a scientist who discovered a way to make himself invisible. Invisibility cloaks have appeared in popular stories like "The Twelve Dancing Princesses" by the Brothers Grimm and J.K. Rowling's Harry Potter series.

The character of Harry Potter uses a magic cloak to make himself invisible in both the books and movies.

## HISTORICAL FACTS

History has stories about invisibility and X-ray-vision superpowers too. Many people have discovered ways to bring humans closer to having these superpowers. One such person was

Wilhelm Conrad Röntgen. Röntgen was a German scientist and mathematician. On November 8, 1895, he discovered the X-ray while working in his laboratory.

Röntgen was experimenting with the flow of an **electric current** through gas in something called a **cathode ray tube**. An electric current is moving electricity. A cathode ray tube is a glass tube with little to no air inside. It has an electric charge running through it. This charge creates a very bright light. Röntgen discovered that if he made some changes to the tube, he could make a new kind of **ray**. A ray is a beam of light. Some rays can be seen by humans while others cannot. He also discovered that if he put something in the path of the new ray, the object would become mostly see-through. When Röntgen placed his own hand and his wife's hand in the path of the ray, he was able to see

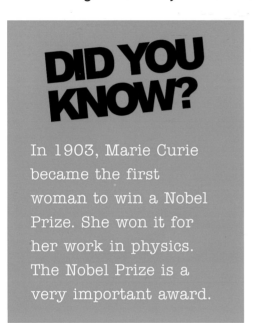

**DID YOU KNOW?**

In 1903, Marie Curie became the first woman to win a Nobel Prize. She won it for her work in physics. The Nobel Prize is a very important award.

bones. Most famously, he could see the bones in his wife's hands, as well as a ring on her finger. This new kind of ray did not have a name. Röntgen called it an X-ray because so little was known about it. He received many awards and medals for his discovery.

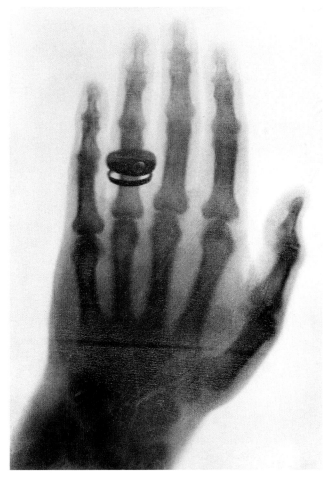

One of the first X-rays showed the bones of Röntgen's wife's hand and a ring she was wearing.

Röntgen's X-ray was studied by scientists all over the world. One of the most well known of these scientists was Marie Curie. She and her husband Pierre lived in France. Pierre was also a scientist. Together, they discovered new **elements**. They also helped people understand more about X-rays. For example, they helped people understand that X-rays are a kind of **radioactivity**.

This photograph shows Marie Curie working in her laboratory in France in 1898.

X-rays give off radiation. In large doses, radiation makes humans very sick. If you ever get an X-ray, the part being X-rayed is exposed to small amounts of radiation. However, the parts of the body not being X-rayed are often covered with a special blanket. This blanket protects those parts from radiation.

After Marie Curie's husband died in 1906, she continued her work. Using her knowledge of radioactivity, she invented small X-ray machines. She and her daughter Irène drove these machines onto battlefields during World War I. They were used to examine injured soldiers. Doctors were able to see bullets and broken bones on the X-ray images. Many soldiers' lives were saved because of Marie Curie's X-ray machines.

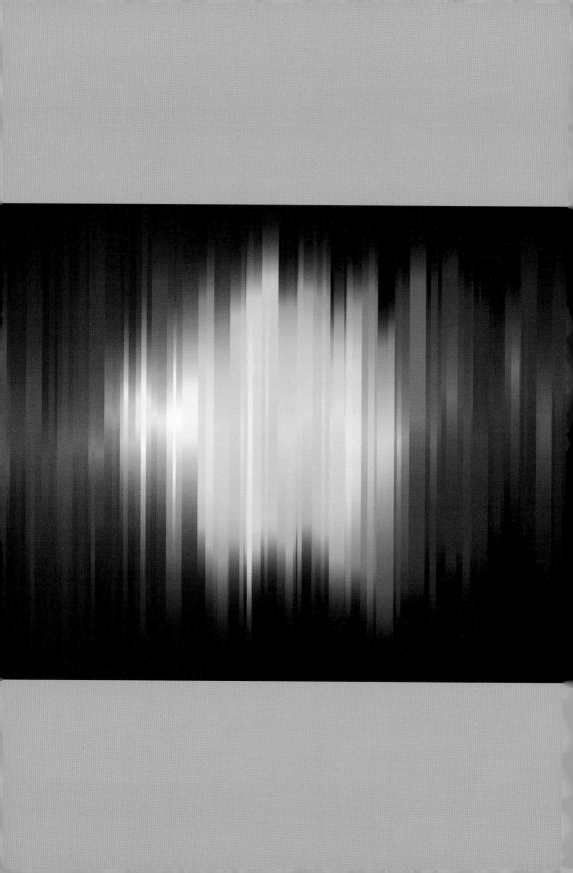

# CHAPTER 2

# SCIENTIFICALLY SPEAKING

U ntil the late 1800s, X-ray vision and invisibility were thought to be impossible for humans. But as we've seen, scientists are figuring out ways to make these abilities possible. But how do these inventions work? How does science make it possible for humans to see through things or appear invisible?

*Opposite*: The only kind of electromagnetic waves that humans can see are called light waves. Light waves allow you to see color.

# THE SCIENCE BEHIND SIGHT

Your eyes can see many different kinds of light. Some kinds of light are harder to see than others. Light from objects like a TV or a **microwave** oven is made up of **electromagnetic waves**.

# Wireless Signals

A new technology being used to create X-ray vision is radio frequency, or RF. Radio frequency works like wireless internet, or Wi-Fi. When you get an X-ray image through wireless signals, it is called RF-Capture. It was first developed at the Massachusetts Institute of Technology in 2015.

When a special RF device is turned on, it sends wireless signals through a wall. The signals will bounce off of the person who is on the other side of the wall and back to the device. The device uses these signals to create an X-ray image of the person in the next room. It can even tell if there is more than one person in the room.

Technology like RF-Capture is still being tested. However, it could be used in the future to improve safety. For example, it could be used to check on small children or the elderly.

An electromagnetic wave is energy made of two parts. One part is an electric field, like static electricity. The other part is a magnetic field, like a refrigerator magnet. When these two fields join together, an electromagnetic wave is created. The only electromagnetic waves humans can see are called light waves.

Light waves allow you to see objects and colors. You can see them because when your eyes are open, they let light in. When light waves hit an object, they bounce off of the object to different parts of your eyes. The eyes' different parts interpret light and color. Tiny parts of the body called **receptors** send messages to other parts of the body. When light waves hit your eye, millions of receptors in your eyes send a message to your brain. They tell your brain what the object is and how it looks. This is how you are able to see and understand what you are looking at.

## THE SCIENCE BEHIND INVISIBILITY

In order to not see something, or for something to appear invisible, it would have to be made of or covered in objects called **metamaterials**. Metamaterials are created by humans. They can do special things that regular materials can't, like make something look invisible. Devices with the right combination of metamaterials can interrupt light waves. If you looked at someone or something covered in metamaterials, they would seem to be invisible. The light that normally passes through your eyes' lenses would be undetectable. The lens is the part of the eye that helps let light in and helps focus on an object. Instead of bouncing off of the person or object you were looking at, the light waves would go right through it. Your eyes would not be able to see the object.

## INVISIBILITY TECHNOLOGY

Inspired by popular stories and science fiction, scientists have tried for years to create an invisibility cloak. Some small cloaks made of metamaterials have been created. When placed in front of an object, the metamaterials interrupt the electromagnetic waves. When the electromagnetic waves are interrupted, the object and the metamaterial cloak covering the object both become invisible. So far, scientists have not created an invisibility cloak big enough for humans.

Another way to create an invisibility effect is to use something called a green screen. A green screen is a large green square that uses the color green to change how the screen's background looks on TV or on a movie theater screen. When viewed on screen, the green background disappears and is replaced with a new background. Green screens are often used by news stations

Green-screen technology is often used to make weather maps appear on TV or to create special visual effects in movies.

to show weather on a map. If someone were to wear a green shirt in front of a green screen, it would appear as though the person's middle was invisible. This effect is also used in movies to create special effects of invisibility.

## THE SCIENCE BEHIND X-RAY VISION

We know that when an X-ray machine is pointed at someone, most X-rays go straight through the body. This is because the body is largely made up

# DID YOU KNOW?

The first pair of X-ray glasses, called X-ray Specs, appeared in 1906. They were sold as toys in comic books and magazines. The X-ray glasses didn't really give you X-ray vision. They changed your vision. However, the idea was popular!

This drawing shows what X-ray glasses could look like.

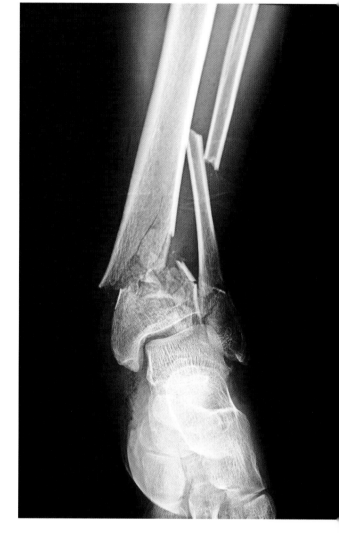

X-rays help doctors find and treat broken bones. This X-ray shows a broken leg.

of muscles and nerves. Muscles and nerves aren't visible in X-rays. However, heavier parts of the body, like bones, are. That is because they do not allow X-rays to pass through them easily. By shining X-rays through your body on special film, the X-rays produce a shadow of the heavier parts of your body. This lets doctors see through patients' bodies. X-rays allow doctors to see things like broken bones so they know the best way to treat patients.

# X-RAY VISION TECHNOLOGY

In addition to an X-ray test at a doctor's office, there are inventions that give humans special eyesight. Night-vision cameras, night-vision

This is how your view mght look if you use night-vision cameras or night-vision goggles.

goggles, and advanced scanning machines are some examples.

Night-vision cameras and goggles take a light ray that is invisible to humans and turn it into a light wave that humans can see. This allows humans to see more detailed images in the dark.

Advanced scanning machines are used at airports to view what is inside luggage without opening it. The luggage passes through a scanning machine. The machine uses microwaves instead of X-rays to see what is inside the luggage. Like X-rays, microwaves are a type of electromagnetic wave. They do not give off as much radiation as X-rays do. This makes them safer to use on airport passengers as well as on luggage.

# CHAPTER 3

# ANIMALS WITH SPECIAL ABILITIES

**W**hile humans haven't developed the superpowers of invisibility or X-ray vision, there are some animals that come close to having these superpowers. Some animals have vision much better than human vision. Other animals can make themselves seem invisible. But how do they do it?

*Opposite*: Chameleons blend into their surroundings so well that they sometimes appear invisible.

# ANIMALS WITH INVISIBLE ABILITIES

The ability to become invisible would be a great superpower for small animals to have. Small animals are often **prey** for larger animals. Prey means larger animals hunt them as food. Small animals could save their lives if they could make themselves invisible when a larger animal was nearby. While they can't make themselves disappear completely, some animals can make themselves blend into their surroundings. In fact, they blend in so well that it is as if they are invisible.

## DID YOU KNOW?

Most **transparent** animals live in water because animals on land need skin with pigment, or natural color, to protect them from the sun's rays.

# HIDDEN FROM VIEW

Many animals on land and in the sea have special abilities to make themselves blend into their surroundings. One example of a land animal that can do this is the chameleon. Chameleons are reptiles. They have scaly skin. This skin is usually the color of their homes. For example, if a chameleon lives in the rain forest, they will be a green color. If they live in the desert, they will be a brown color.

Most chameleons are found in rain forests and deserts in Africa. Chameleon skin has a layer of pigment, or natural color. Under that layer of skin are special **cells**, or tiny units, with small crystals.

Cuttlefish often appear invisible. Can you find the cuttlefish in this photo?

When chameleons move the spacing between these crystals, it causes the light waves to change. When the light waves change, the chameleon's skin color changes. Changing colors is how chameleons communicate and how they keep warm or cool. Their colors also help them hide

# The Glasswing Butterfly

The glasswing butterfly is a type of butterfly that lives in Central America. It is called the glasswing butterfly because its wings are transparent, or see-through. The wings have tiny bumps that act like metamaterial. These bumps cause rays of light to pass through the wing, making them invisible. These invisible wings help the glasswing butterfly hide from predators. It is difficult for predators to spot a butterfly with invisible wings while the butterfly is flying.

The glasswing butterfly has wings that are see-through, like glass.

from animals that want to eat them.

A sea animal that blends in well with its environment is the cuttlefish. Unlike the chameleon, the cuttlefish doesn't stay in areas that match its coloring. Instead, the cuttlefish can change its shape and colors to blend in with its surroundings. This makes it seem invisible. Cuttlefish skin has millions of color cells in it. These color cells can create different color patterns. This allows the cuttlefish to hide from **predators** or to sneak up on its prey. Cuttlefish also have special muscles that allow them to change shape. They can disguise themselves as rocks or algae under the sea to make themselves invisible to other animals.

Other sea creatures that can hide themselves from predators are the glass octopus and the glass squid. The glass octopus has a body that is almost entirely transparent, or see-through, like glass. This transparency makes them almost invisible to predators. The glass octopus has eyes

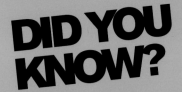

DID YOU KNOW?

Cats' eyes glow in the dark because they have a special reflective area at the back of their eyes. This area seems to glow when light hits it.

The glass squid has a body that is see-through, making it appear almost invisible.

and organs that can still be seen, even though most of its body cannot. To make itself even more invisible to predators, the glass octopus positions itself in certain ways. For example, it positions itself so that its eyes and organs show little to no shadow on the ocean floor. Without a shadow to guide them, predators often do not see the glass octopus. Like the glass octopus, the glass squid also has eyes that are not transparent, even though its body is. To disguise its eyes, it uses special organs underneath them. These special organs create a light that looks a lot like sunlight streaming through the ocean. When predators look at the glass squid, all they see is the light. They mistake the light for the sun. They do not see the glass squid's eyes or transparent body. The glass squid has made itself invisible to its predators.

## ANIMALS WITH SPECIAL SIGHT

While no animals have the power of X-ray vision, there are many animals that do have special eyesight. One animal is a common pet, the cat. Cats have very sensitive eyesight. They do not need as much light as humans to see. Cats' eyes are similar to night-vision cameras and goggles. They are able to see in the dark as well as in the light. This is because their eyes have larger lenses than human eyes. With larger lenses, cats' eyes can let more light in. Cats' eyes also have two types of cells. One type of cell works in bright light. The other type of cell works in dim light. These cells

Cats' eyes have large lenses and special cells that give them very sensitive eyesight.

allow cats to see during the day and at night. Cats' night vision means that they can go hunting at night for prey, like mice.

Another animal with special eyesight is the carpenter bee. Carpenter bees can see well during the day. They can also see very well at night. This is because carpenter bees have special cells in their eyes that absorb light during the day. Multiple cells send a lot of light to their brain at one time. This gives the bees' eyes a powerful boost of light and very good vision at night.

Carpenter bees have good daytime and nighttime vision.

# CHAPTER 4

# EXPLORING THE FUTURE

T oday, scientists continue to study the science behind superpowers like invisibility and X-ray vision. What new technology might be created in the future to bring humans closer to these superpowers? How might humans use invisibility and X-ray vision in the future?

*Opposite*: Will smartphones be used as personal X-ray devices in the future?

or invisibility, device to use on their cars. Toyota would like to use this new technology to make driving safer. They want to make parts of their cars appear invisible to those in the driver's seat. Today, some parts of the front of a car are needed for safety. Those parts can also block the driver's view. Toyota's cloaking device would allow drivers to see through parts that are normally in the way. Having

Scientists are working to make cars safer by making some parts of the car invisible.

invisible parts would help drivers see other cars on the road and people walking nearby more clearly. As Toyota continues to develop and start using this new technology, it is possible we will see cars with invisible parts in the future.

In addition to cars, scientists and engineers are working to make planes appear invisible on radar. Radar is a device that lets you know when an object is close. It works by sending out bursts of radio waves. The radio waves bounce off of any objects in the sky and back to the radar. The bigger an object is, the more radio waves will bounce back to the radar. This makes it possible to estimate the size of an object in the sky.

This is what it looks like when an airport security system examines luggage under their special scanner.

had access to their own, safe X-ray device, then people would be less likely to skip important health tests. Illnesses would be found sooner, and more lives could be saved. Maybe taking X-rays at home will be a common habit in the future.

While humans probably won't develop the superpowers of invisibility or X-ray vision any time soon, scientists keep working to create devices that can make these superpowers real. As technology continues to improve, it is possible that invisibility cloaks and X-ray glasses may eventually be part of people's everyday lives.

# GLOSSARY

**CATHODE RAY TUBE** A tube with little air and an electric charge that causes a very bright light.

**CELLS** Very small units in the body that perform many functions, like absorbing light in the eyes.

**ELECTRIC CURRENT** A flow of electricity, like static electricity, a lightning bolt, or a battery.

**ELECTROMAGNETIC WAVE** A wave of energy made up of an electric field and a magnetic field.

**ELEMENT** Made up of only one kind of atom and can't be broken down into a different kind of matter.

**METAMATERIALS** Nonnatural materials made by humans and used to make objects appear invisible.

**MICROWAVE** A type of electromagnetic wave.

**NANO-ANTENNA** A tiny antenna that can change wavelengths.

**PHILOSOPHY** The study of knowledge and reasoning or a certain way of thinking.

**PREDATOR** An animal that hunts other animals.

**PREY** An animal hunted by another animal.

**RADIATION** Waves of energy that may be harmful to humans.

**RADIOACTIVITY** The release of radiation or chemicals that release radiation.

**RAY** A beam of light that may or may not be seen by humans.

**RECEPTORS** Cells that send a message to your brain.

**TRANSPARENT** Something that you can see through, like glass.

# FIND OUT MORE

## BOOKS

Resler, T.J. *How Things Work: Discover Secrets and Science Behind Bounce Houses, Hovercraft, Robotics, and Everything in Between*. Washington, DC: National Geographic Children's Books, 2016.

Stine, Megan. *Who Was Marie Curie?* New York: Grosset & Dunlap, 2014.

Woodford, Chris. *Science: A Visual Encyclopedia*. New York: DK Publishing, 2014.

# WEBSITES

**Ducksters Physics for Kids: Types of Electromagnetic Waves**

http://www.ducksters.com/science/physics/types_of_electromagnetic_waves.php

This is a page dedicated to learning about different types of electromagnetic waves, including microwaves, radio waves, and X-rays.

**How Do Green Screens Work?**

https://www.livescience.com/55814-how-do-green-screens-work.html

This website explores the magic of a green screen and explains how it works.

**Mocomi (Motion Comics for Kids)**

http://mocomi.com/x-rays

This page features an animated video explaining how X-rays work.

# INDEX

# ABOUT THE AUTHOR

**Kaitlin Scirri** received her bachelor's of arts degree in writing from State University of New York College at Buffalo State. In addition to writing, she is also an editor with a special interest in children's books. Her favorite part of researching this book was learning about Marie Curie's contributions to treating wounded soldiers during World War I with the invention of her small, mobile X-ray machines.